Published by Hallmark Gift Books,
a division of Hallmark Cards, Inc.
Kansas City, MO 64141
Visit us on the Web at Hallmark.com.

Editorial Director: Carrie Bolin
Editor: Lindsay Evans
Art Director: Chris Opheim
Designers: Rich LaPierre & Dan Horton
Production Designer: Dan Horton

ISBN: 978-1-59530-758-3
IXKT1634

Printed and bound in China
JUL15

A Charlie Brown CHRISTMAS

by CHARLES M. SCHULZ

Adapted by Lindsay Evans
Art adapted by Rich LaPierre & Dan Horton
Based on the television special produced and directed by Lee Mendelson and Bill Melendez.

Hallmark

Christmastime had arrived—a time when

snow fell softly to the earth and carols rang sweetly in the air. It was a time filled with cheer—a time when everyone was happy. Everyone, of course, except for Charlie Brown.

He decided his friend Lucy might be able to help him.

"You need to get involved in some real Christmas project," she said. "How would you like to be the director of our Christmas play?"

Charlie Brown knew nothing about being a director, but Lucy was pretty convincing.

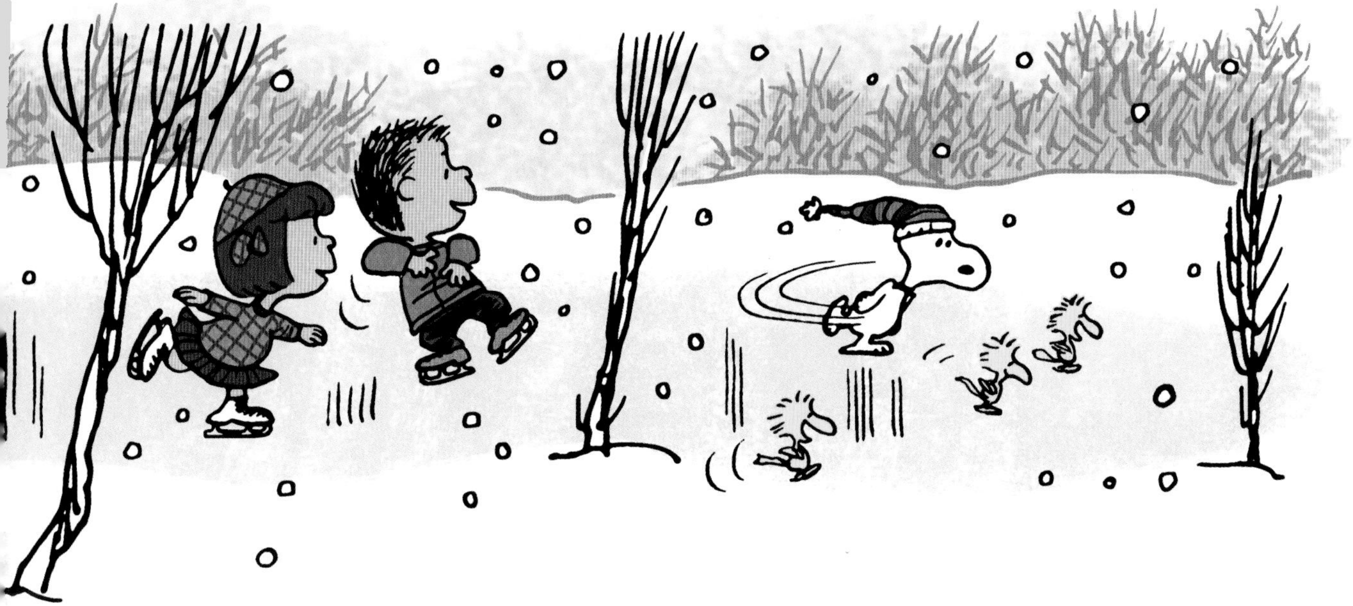

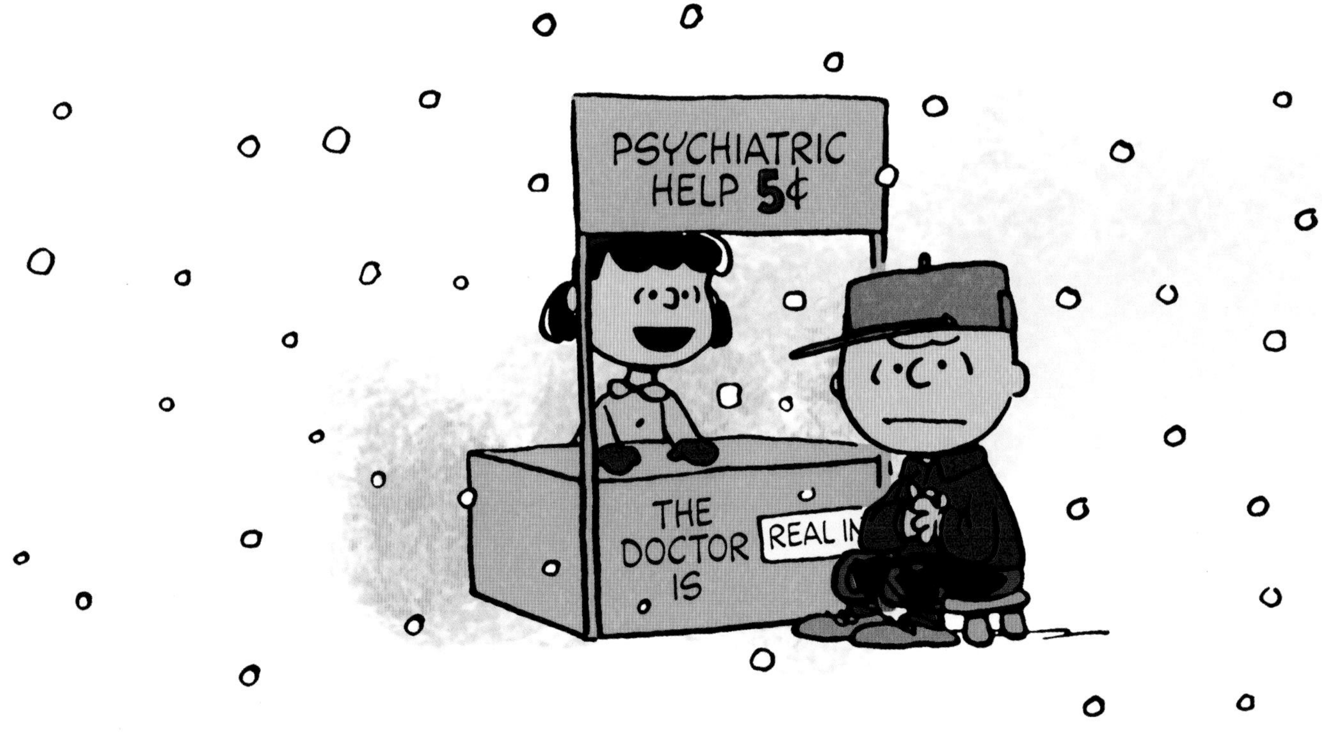

PSYCHIATRIC HELP 5¢
THE DOCTOR IS
REAL IN

Charlie Brown headed to the auditorium and ran into his dog, Snoopy, carrying a box of Christmas decorations.

"What's going on here?" asked Charlie Brown.

Snoopy handed him a flier, which read: "Find the true meaning of Christmas. Win money, money, money at the super-colossal lights-and-display contest!"

Charlie Brown couldn't believe his eyes. "My own dog has gone commercial!"

In the auditorium, the kids danced around the stage to upbeat jazz music.

"Places, everybody. Let's rehearse!" yelled Charlie Brown, but everyone just continued dancing.

"Good grief," he said. This was all wrong. They needed the proper mood for their performance. "We need a Christmas tree," he announced.

"Hey," said Lucy. "A great big, shiny aluminum Christmas tree. That's it, Charlie Brown! You get the tree. I'll handle this crowd."

The Christmas tree lot was full to bursting with shiny metallic trees in every color imaginable. "Gee, do they still make wooden trees?" asked Linus.

Just then, Charlie Brown set his eyes on a scraggly, sad, little pine tree. "This one here seems to need a home," he said. "It will be just right for our play. Besides, I think it needs me."

They carried the little tree into the auditorium, but no one liked it. "Everything I do turns into a disaster," said Charlie Brown with a sigh. "I guess I really don't know what Christmas is all about. Isn't there anyone who knows what Christmas is all about?"

"Sure," said Linus. "I can tell you what Christmas is all about."

A dim spotlight shone down on Linus, and he said: "There were shepherds in the field, keeping watch over their flock by night. The angel said unto them, 'Fear not, for behold, I bring you tidings of great joy, which will be to all people. For unto you is born this day a Savior, Christ the Lord.' And suddenly, there was with the angel a multitude of heavenly host, praising God and saying, 'Glory to God in the highest, and on Earth peace, goodwill toward men.'"

Linus picked up his blanket and walked back to his friend. "That's what Christmas is all about, Charlie Brown."

Charlie Brown picked up his sad little tree and smiled. "Linus is right," he said. "I won't let commercialism ruin my Christmas. I'll take this tree home and decorate it, and I'll show them it really will work in our play."

Charlie Brown passed Snoopy's doghouse and picked up a shiny, red ornament to hang on his tree.

He frowned as the little tree bent under the weight. "I've killed it!" Charlie Brown cried. "Everything I touch gets ruined!"

Charlie Brown's friends came outside and saw the wilted tree. "I never thought it was such a bad little tree," said Linus as he straightened it and wrapped his blanket around the base. "It just needs a little love."

The kids took the other ornaments and lights off Snoopy's doghouse and began to decorate the tree. It transformed into a beautiful sight, and when Charlie Brown came back, he hardly recognized it.

"Merry Christmas, Charlie Brown!" shouted his friends, and then they began to sing.

Charlie Brown's friends came outside and saw the wilted tree. "I never thought it was such a bad little tree," said Linus as he straightened it and wrapped his blanket around the base. "It just needs a little love."

The kids took the other ornaments and lights off Snoopy's doghouse and began to decorate the tree. It transformed into a beautiful sight, and when Charlie Brown came back, he hardly recognized it.

"Merry Christmas, Charlie Brown!" shouted his friends, and then they began to sing.

If you have enjoyed this book
or it has touched your life in some way,
we would love to hear from you.

Please send your comments to:
Hallmark Book Feedback
P.O. Box 419034
Mail Drop 100
Kansas City, MO 64141

Or e-mail us at:
booknotes@hallmark.com